Carr's
DICTIONARY OF
Extra-Ordinary Cricketers

W. G. Grace

A young J.L. Carr leaves home for teacher training college,
watched by his father – with the essential accessory of
a cricket bat strapped to his luggage.

Carr's
DICTIONARY
OF
Extra-Ordinary
Cricketers

J.L. CARR

with illustrations by the author

A QUINCE TREE PRESS BOOK

J.L. Carr's novels, little books and maps are
available from the Quince Tree Press, 116 Hardwick Lane,
Bury St Edmunds, Suffolk IP33 2LE, 01284 753228,
www.quincetreepress.co.uk

This book is dedicated to MRS TURNER, of East Hoathly, Sussex, who in 1739 wrote in a letter, '*Last Munday my dear husband plaid at cricket & came home pleased anuf for he struck the best ball in the game and whisht he had not annything else to do he would play Cricket all his life.*'

And also to DIANA WALKER, Form Va, Colchester High School, who in the school magazine wrote, '*Cricket is the most boring game in existence and is as dreadful for players as spectators. Nothing happens but monotonous bangs and remarks. After two or three days when everyone has forgotten the beginning, it ends in a draw.*'

And to ABDUL AZIZ, known also as Abdul the Damned, Turkish potentate, who, witnessing English soldiers playing cricket, exclaimed, '*Remarkable! But what needless exertion! Why do you not compel your slaves and concubines to perform it for you?*'

And to those cricketers thronging shadowy fields far from home and we who loved them.

We fall like the leaves of the tree,
And we go.
Even we,
Even so.

First published in Great Britain
1977 by J.L. Carr, The Quince Tree Press

Published in an expanded edition 1983
by Quartet Books/Solo Books

This new edition published 2005 by Aurum Press Ltd
25 Bedford Avenue, London WC1B 3AT
in association with the Quince Tree Press

A catalogue record for this book is available
from the British Library.

ISBN 1 84513 081 2

1 3 5 7 9 10 8 6 4 2
2005 2007 2009 2008 2006

Designed and typeset in Caslon by Peter Ward
Printed by MPG Books, Bodmin, Cornwall

Contents

Introduction

BY

MATTHEW ENGEL

Mention the name J.L. Carr to a well-read English adult, and you evoke one of two reactions: either a blank stare or that look of delight that comes from anyone who has just met a fellow-devotee of someone or something obscure, from an unknown artist to an esoteric sexual taste.

He is best-known as a novelist, but summing Jim Carr up in a word just diminishes him. Every writer is necessarily unique, but some are more unique than others. And there never has, and never will be, a writer remotely like him.

He was born in Yorkshire in 1912, and until he was 55 was simply the headmaster of a primary school in Kettering, which is a much-overlooked town in Northamptonshire, itself often regarded as England's most forgettable county. But Jim was never simply anything: he was a man of extraordinary complexity: a teacher of startling originality, cartographer, batik artist, patron of wood engraving, stone carver, church-lover, London-loather . . .

All this enabled him to produce, between middle age

and old age, eight novels – several of which deserve to be read as long as the language lasts – twenty books of wood engravings, forty wonderfully idiosyncratic county maps, two 'inflammatory evangelical tracts' and eighty-odd 'small books'. Most of these works, including the two last novels, he published himself, from his back bedroom in Kettering.

The small books really were small: most were 16 pages worth of filleted poetry, barely the size of an inflammatory tract, that would fit in the tiniest pocket, and be afforded by the meanest one. Carr the businessman (that was one of his many unwriterly skills) cottoned on to the fact that you could, with some difficulty, persuade booksellers to put these mini-works by the till to be sold for a pittance as an impulse buy. Supermarkets put sweeties by the checkout on the same principle. And bigger publishers than him cottoned on this. In the 1990s Penguin began a brief craze for 60p booklets that looked likely to transform the entire publishing trade until the market became saturated and readers realised that even 60p was expensive if you were never going to read the wretched thing. And these days improbable mega-stores selling records and DVDs will stick a few Christmas-type pot-boilers on the counter to pick up casual sales from people who never go near a conventional book shop.

Carr invented the idea in 1964 to mark the centenary of the death of John Clare, arguably the only other great writer to draw inspiration from Northamptonshire. He came to know a lot about public taste, as he later told his biographer, Byron Rogers: '. . . Blake being his bestseller, followed by Shakespeare, Clare and Donne, but Milton and Dryden he could not give away to their countrymen.'

He also told Rogers that the series enabled him to publish his own favourite poet, James Elroy Flecker, and to put in his introduction: 'He wrote one memorable line

> *Their bosoms shame the roses; their behinds*
> *Impel the astonished nightingales to sing*

but then struck it out.' I am not a Flecker man myself, but that sentence is quintessential Carr. It is fascinating, funny, a bit naughty, and you find yourself scratching your head and wondering where the hell he got that.

'These books,' Carr would write inside the back cover, 'hover between a greeting and a present. They fit a common envelope and go for minimum postage. In cold bedrooms, only one hand to the wrist need suffer exposure . . .'

In 1977 he expanded the genre to produce *Carr's Dictionary of Extra-Ordinary* (even that hyphen is Carrish) *English Cricketers*. This comprised 126 entries from Dr Arthur Abraham to I. Zingari. It was later expanded to allow another 80. This caught the public fancy even more than Blake or Shakespeare. It came at a time when cricket, and the English idyll it represents, was becoming briefly fashionable again, a reaction – I think –

against the notion of 'progress', which in the 1960s had been widely believed to be unstoppable.

Cricket was always important to Jim. He was, by all accounts, a very decent club batsman. The first public hint of his literary talent had come in the 1950s when he edited the yearbook of the Northamptonshire County Cricket League and wrote introductions of a mastery that must have left the readers either enchanted, bewildered or both.

All his novels represent some fragment of his life, and his second novel, published in 1967, *A Season in Sinji*, covered both his war service – spent on a Godforsaken flying-boat base in West Africa – and his cricket. He caught the twists and turns of the game beautifully, even elegaically, and manipulated them into a metaphor for life. It is the best cricket novel ever written.

But even that never had the appeal of *Extra-Ordinary Cricketers*. 'It was a series of facts about cricketers, most of them long dead,' explained Rogers. 'Also about five women, two dogs and a horse.' The horse is Horace (see page 36). Some of the entries are vague and seemingly uncontestable:

> CHARLES JESSE KORTRIGHT, Essex, b. 1891, by aficionados said to have been the fastest bowler of them all . . .

Others are more specific.

HESKETH K. NAYLER, *c.* 1851, a New York millionaire impotent who derived sexual gratification by maintaining an establishment of ample women to play cricket before him with balloons and without clothes.

Cricketers' lives have always been a matter of interest. *Wisden* has been publishing regular obituaries since 1892, which may have been too late for Nayler, who presumably died of excitement some time before then. Footballers' lives are hardly ever extra-ordinary. But the nature of cricket, and the time it takes, tends to attract extra-ordinary figures and bring out their extra-ordinary qualities. The very first page of obituaries in the 2005 *Wisden* contains both Anthony Ainley and Bill Alley.

Ainley was an actor who played the Master in *Dr Who* but was also 'an eccentric and very effective opening bat who appeared in full body padding, sunblock, helmet and swimming goggles' and always took his teas alone in his car, possibly because 'he despised cheeses of all kinds'. Alley of Somerset, at the peak at his batting form, would tell bowlers where to move their fielders and, if they complied, smash the ball over the chap's head regardless. As editor, I feel I am consciously carrying on the Carr tradition. There is a slight difference since *Wisden* has stern fact-checkers who would doubtless point out that, if Kortright really had been born in 1891, he would have made his debut for Essex at the age of two.

But, with Jim, none of this matters. In his novels, there is always a heavy dose of reality. In his dictionaries, imagination can take over wherever the trail of facts peters out. *Cricketers* was followed by such works as *English Kings, Consorts, Pretenders, Usurpers, Unnatural Claimants and Royal Athelings*. I have just looked up 'atheling' (*obs*, OE, 'a member of a noble family' – SOED) for what must be the fifteenth time because I always forget it and refuse to believe that anyone except Carr has used it in the past century.

I would love to find my copy of the dictionary too, just as I'd love to consult *Prelates, Parsons, Vergers, Wardens, Sidesmen and Preachers, Sunday-School Teachers, Hermits, Ecclesiastical Flower-Arrangers, Fifth Monarchy Men and False Prophets*. The problem is finding them. Because these slim volumes have no spine, they cannot be displayed on a shelf. They may allow one hand to stay warm in cold bedrooms. But they also disappear into crannies and dusty corners, down the sides of sofas and under piles of papers. Some booksellers found this a problem, but it is an even greater problem to all but the most methodical book-collector. One is inclined to suspect that this was all part of Carr's business master plan: a form of built-in obsolescence, forcing the enthusiast to re-purchase the books at frequent intervals.

So here, in a more cherishable format, are Carr's collected Extra-ordinary Cricketers. They should alert a new generation to its author's genius, and lead on to an appreciation, not just of Athelings and Flower-Arrangers, but of the novels as well.

J.L. Carr died in 1994. I had the honour of publishing his last piece, the 1993 *Wisden* book review, which he ended with the very Carrish sentence: 'My aunt was not present on either occasion.' His reputation will endure, I am certain of that. As much as anyone mentioned in the glorious pages that follow, he was an extra-ordinary man.

Matthew Engel

2005

Carr's

DICTIONARY

OF

Extra-Ordinary
Cricketers

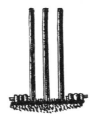

A

DR ARTHUR ABRAHAM, b. 1889, so resembled his twin, a heavy run-getter, that opponents frequently complained to umpires that he had already batted.

CHARLES ABSOLON scored 1,029 runs and took 103 wkts in his seventy-second year. At the age of seventy-eight he twice performed the hat-trick.

CAPTAIN ADAMSON, *c.* 1844, having deserted his place on the boundary at Phoenix Park, Dublin, to converse with a lady, sprang back over a four-foot spiked fence and, while in the air, took a left-handed catch.

THERE'S NO CATCH IN IT.

CAPTAIN ADAMSON PLAYING IN DUBLIN, JUMPED A SPIKED IRON FENCE, 4 FEET HIGH. WHILST IN THE AIR HE MADE THE CATCH LEFT-HANDED. THE BATSMAN WAS **W.G.GRACE.**

SULTAN ABDUL AZIZ
(ABDUL THE DAMNED) WATCHING HIS FIRST
GAME, EXCLAIMED "WONDERFUL .... BUT
WHY DON'T YOU MAKE YOUR SERVANTS
DO THIS FOR YOU ??"

G.O. ALLEN, b. Sydney, 1902. Cambridge University, Middlesex and England Captain, President of M.C.C. In 1929 this fine fast bowler took all 10 Lancashire wkts in an innings for 40 runs.

E.B. ALLETSON, Notts., during ninety minutes of 1911, made 189 runs out of a partnership of 227. Playing himself in with a careful 47 in his first fifty minutes, he then added 142 between 2.15 p.m. and 2.55 p.m., treating Killick particularly severely. (56 in two overs).

Mr H.S. Altham, a Winchester housemaster, in 1926 published the most satisfying history of the game. Mr E.W. Swanton later collaborated in this great work.

W.E. Astill, Leics., b. 1888, the archetypal backbone of any county side. From 1906 until 1939, he took 2,500 wkts and made 23,000 runs. He also played the ukulele.

Karl Auty, *c.* 1911, a Chicago insomniac, had a joiner make him an under-bed shelf on runners to accommodate his set of *Wisdens*.

James Aylward, *c.* 1770, Hambledon, a left-handed farm labourer, who made 167 for the village against All-England. Sir Horace Mann lured him to Kent with promise of preferment but he did not fulfil early promise either as batsman or bailiff.

B

BACELLI, the ravishingly lovely mistress of the Eton schoolboy Duke of Dorset who, in 1754, was dismissed from his favours after running him out.

MR H. BAGSHAW, Derbyshire, d. 1902, asked that his umpire's coat, containing six pebbles, should be his shroud.

A.H. BAKEWELL, Northants., b. 1908, returning from making 241* against the 1936 Champion County, Derbyshire, had an accident on the road, and never again played first-class cricket.

MRS BARLOW, wife of the cricketer R. Barlow (*see also* HORNBY), ruefully described herself to a neighbour as the unpaid curator of a cricket museum.

S.F. BARNES, b. Smethwick, 1873, an erect and uncompromisingly hostile fast-medium bowler who, using variations of his inswinger which straightened on pitching, took 189 Test Match wkts at an average of 16.43. Cricket was his occupation and most of his career was spent as a well-paid destroyer in leagues where he took 4,000 wkts at an average of 7. Cognoscenti declare him to have been the greatest bowler of all time. At the age of fifty-six, playing for the Minor Counties v. S. Africa, he took 8 wkts for 4 runs. He was a free-thinker, declaring, *'When I'm bowling, there's only one captain, Me!'* He was not particularly popular amongst players but A.C. MacLaren probably overstated his dislike when, during a storm at sea, he philosophically remarked, *'Well, there's one comfort. If we go down, that b***** Barnes will go down with us.'*

W. BATES, Yorks. b. 1855, a dashing bat, medium pace off-break bowler, and much admired baritone singer at smokers. His rendering of that moving song, 'The Bonny Yorkshire Lass', was particularly popular and, during the season of 1879, he married one. Whereupon, Edmund Peate (1,923 wkts at 13.2) sourly remarked, *'Baates is nobbut a fooil. 'E should ha' got issel wed id middle o' winter so as 'e cud ha gi'en his oondivided attention t' it.'*

THE REVD. LORD FREDERICK BEAUCLERK, D.D., Vicar of St Albans, *c.* 1820, great-grandson of King Charles II and Nell Gwynne and known in the Soho district as Fred Diamond Eye. This choleric man took his stand at the wicket wearing a scarlet sash and a white beaver and demonstrated his contempt for

REV. LORD FREDERICK BEAUCLERK, D.D
KNOWN TO LES GIRLS AS 'FRED DIAMOND-EYE'.

HE USED TO BOAST THAT HE MADE £2,000 A YEAR FROM BETS ON GAMES IN WHICH HE PLAYED AND OFTEN SHOWED HIS SCORN FOR CERTAIN FAST BOWLERS BY HANGING HIS **GOLD WATCH** ON THE MIDDLE STUMP

some bowlers by suspending a valuable gold watch from his middle stump. He is said to have been an unutterably dull preacher.

MAX BEERBOHM, b. 1872, a much admired Edwardian writer who subscribed a shilling to W. G. Grace's Testimonial *'not in support of cricket but as an earnest protest against golf'*.

WILLIAM BELDHAM, *c.* 1770, of Wrecclesham, Surrey and Hambledon, known also as Silver Billy, one of cricket's patriarchs in the Glorious Dawn of the Game, whose late cut presented so noble a spectacle it was said that only Michelangelo could have delineated it with justice. Only his lapse in biasing the ball with a lump of clay causing it to violently swerve and dismiss Lord Beauclerk can be said to sully his lustrous name. His vigour continued unimpaired until he forsook this life for immortality *aetat.*

ninety-six, mourned by the twenty-eight children of his first wife and eleven more amassed in a second innings.

BLACK BESS OF THE MINT, *c.* 1744, frequently engaged to enliven dull Spitalfields games by running foot races without drawers against Little Bit o' Blue, a Stepney person.

EDMUND BLUNDEN, b. 1896, the poet, whose essays in *Cricket Country* are a most charming evocation of Kent village cricket.

COLIN BLYTHE, Kent, b. 1879, a subtle left-arm spin bowler, who in fifteen seasons took 2,506 wkts averaging 16. On a single day in 1907, he took 17 Northamptonshire wkts for 48 runs. He was killed on the Western Front in 1917.

JOHN BOOT, d. 1737 in a collision at Newark with his batting partner.

B.J.T. BOSANQUET, Mddx., b. 1877, (whose great-grandniece works in this office) having secretly invented the googly at tishy-toshy first unveiled it in the presence of the great Victor Trumper and immediately dismissed him.

IAN BOTHAM, Somerset, b. 1955, an all-round cricketer, unbelievably born in Cheshire, who, though dwelling amongst us in these drab days, unquestionably belongs to cricket's Golden Age. His peers are Spofforth, Trumper, Hurst, Jessop, and all that Happy Throng. It was of him that the poet Shelley prophesied:

> *He has outsoared the shadow of our night;*
> *From the contagion of our world's slow stain.*
> *He is secure. The soul of Adonais like a star*
> *Beams from the abode where the eternal are.*

W.E. BOWES, Yorks., b. 1908, a fast bowler, rose to twin pinnacles of fame. In his only 1932 Test in Australia, he

bowled Bradman for 0 and, in 1946 at Chesterfield, brought relief to his fellow toilers by discovering that the pitch was twenty-four yards long.

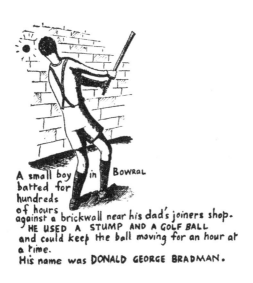

A small boy in BOWRAL batted for hundreds of hours against a brickwall near his dad's joiners shop. HE USED A STUMP AND A GOLF BALL and could keep the ball moving for an hour at a time.
His name was DONALD GEORGE BRADMAN.

L.C. BRAUND, Surrey, Somerset, d. 1955, who in the 1903 Test series made 102, took 8 for 81 and, running from slip, took a catch at fine leg from the bowling of Hirst.

J. BRIGGS, Lancs., b. 1862, played for that county in his seventeenth year. This Northamptonshire-born all-rounder was a man of such inexhaustible stamina that he played an innings of 186 on the first day of his honeymoon.

Harry calmly whipped off the bails, yelled "'Ow's zat?" and the umpire gave him out.

C. BROWN, the Notts. wicket-keeper, known also as Mad Charlie, an out-of-season dye vat mixer, dared not be approached by either management or trade-union organisers because of his excitable and highly dramatic reconstruction of stumpings and appeals.

GEORGE BROWN, Hants., d. 1964, perhaps momentarily inflamed by his own striking resemblance to a Red Indian chief, flung himself into the path of a

Hobbs off-drive. When the ball was prised from this brave man's fingers, it was discovered that its manufacturer's gilt trademark and address (in reverse) was embossed upon his palm.

GEORGE BROWN, Surrey, b. Stoughton, 1783, a sixteen-stone underarm bowler of such ferocity that a wicket-keeper and two longstops (one wearing a sack of straw) were customary. Even so, one delivery passing through the coat held out by the second longstop, killed instantly a large and valuable dog.

F. BUCKLE, Mddx., v. Surrey, 1869; score read:
1st inns – not sent for in time – 0
2nd inns – absent unwell – 0

H.E. BULL, *c.* 1864 for M.C.C. v. Oxford University, the first recorded player to be martyred under Law 37 which prohibits a second hit at the same ball.

Julius Caesar, *natus* Godalming, *circa* MLCCCXXIX, a slow bowler who, on overseas tours, wept if required to sleep alone. He later was coach at Uppingham.

EHEU, POSTUME, FUGACES LABU

DID **JULIUS CÆSAR** PLAY FOR THE **M.C.C.?** YES! BUT **NOT** THE CAPTAIN OF LEGIONS. **J. CÆSAR** PLAYED FOR ENGLAND AGAINST AMERICA IN **1859**. HE WAS A SURREY MAN AND DISLIKED SLEEPING ALONE IN STRANGE BEDS.

Sir Julius Cahn, *c.* 1944, a Nottinghamshire millionaire furnisher, wore inflatable pads and, when playing on his private ground, usually was given leg-byes as runs.

NEVILLE CARDUS, b. 1889, a writer whose match reports for the Manchester *Guardian* adorn literature, and properly earned him knighthood. He chose as his World XI, Hobbs, Trumper, Bradman, Macartney, F.S. Jackson (Capt.), Faulkner, Miller, Rhodes, Oldfield, Larwood, Barnes.

C.C. CASE, Somerset, 1930, having fallen upon his wickets after a delivery from Voce of Notts., was so distressed that he arrived back at the pavilion carrying a stump.

A.P.F. CHAPMAN, Cambridge University, Berkshire and Kent, d. 1961, captained England in six successive Test victories. When young, this Adonis was a nonpareil at cover and, later, a telescopic gulley catcher. His sad, last years do not bear remembering so let him forever lead out his 1930 side at Headingley – Hobbs, Sutcliffe, Hammond, Duleepsinghi, Larwood . . . ah!

JOHN CHITTY's bat, hewn in 1729, is cricket's earliest archaeological artefact.

SIR WINSTON CHURCHILL did not play cricket.

CHARLES CLARKE, the liveliest cricket literary ghost whose felicitous style elevated John Nyren's reminiscences into a sublime masterpiece.

WILLIAM CLARKE, Notts., b. 1798, a one-eyed bricklayer of parsonic demeanour who founded Trent Bridge, was the first managerial entrepreneur and is said to have played *by ear*. He bowled rearing underarm breakbacks whose difficulty was exacerbated by his shrill cry of, '*We shall 'ave a haccident, sir, in a moment!*' He is the earliest example of an unhappily enduring line of odious captains with rooted dislike of taking themselves off.

TOM CLEMENT, *c.* 1750, Alton, fell under cricket's subtle spell aged five. The Revd. Gilbert White (*see* Eng. Lit. *also* Nat. Hist.) wrote, '*Tom bats, his grand-mother bowls, and his great-grandmother watches out.*'

F.C. COBDEN, Cambridge University, performed a hat-trick when, in 1870, Oxford needed but 2 to win. This feat had so profound an effect on all who witnessed it that the occasion is still known reverently as Cobden's Match.

LORD COBHAM, President of M.C.C., batting for the Band of Brothers v. Bluemantles, exulted when shattering glass confirmed that his hit had cleared the Tunbridge Wells pavilion. But later, hastening to his car to take news of this feat to his wife, he found the windscreen in fragments.

THE WORLD'S **TOP SCORE** WAS MADE BY ARTHUR COLLINS, AGED 14. HE SCORED 628 NOT OUT. IN A HOUSE MATCH AT CLIFTON COLLEGE IN 1899. HIS SUBSEQUENT CAREER IS UNKNOWN TO FAME.

MASTER A.E.J. COLLINS, Clifton School, was aged thirteen years when, in an 1899 housematch that dragged on for several games afternoons and lunchtimes, he amassed the highest recorded score of 628* in six hours, fifty-nine minutes and was only deterred from adding to this splendid total by the expostulations of spectators and the threats of those still waiting to bat.

DENIS COMPTON, Mddx., and England, b. 1918, although a batsman of genius, sometimes was so uncertain a runner that it was said a call from him was no more than a basis for negotiation.

MRS ALICE CONSTANTINE, a deeply religious person, who when her son Learie was carried home with a cracked kneebone, remarked, 'They who live by the sword shall perish by the sword.'

THE REVD. FRANCIS CORNFORD, Vicar of Cam, *c.* 1863, batting on Stinchcombe Ridge, Glos., made a hit yielding 18 runs. '*Lost Ball!*' could not be called because at no time was the ball out of sight.

ARTHUR COURCEY, Epsom, a stockbroker, a spectator of the 1882 Oval Test, which England lost by 7 runs. While enduring thirteen successive maiden overs he gnawed off the handle of his brother-in-law's umbrella.

THE HON. CHARLES COVENTRY, who toured South Africa with Major Warton's 1889 side, customarily went in last man and never bowled. Several years later during the ill-advised Jameson Raid, a friend, having seen him laid out under a blanket and kicking like a shot hare, misreported him dead. Arriving at the Warwickshire family chapel during his memorial service, he was so entranced by the tributes to his memory that he invited the mourners to a dance on the village green and then to a modest banquet on the funeral meats. He continued alive until 1924.

AT AN M.C.C MEETING IN 1902 THE WIDTH OF THE BOWLING CREASE WAS INCREASED FROM 6'6" TO 6'8". ONLY A REV. J. C. CRAWFORD OBJECTED. But he would give no REASON!

THE REVD. J.G. CRAWFORD was the only objector to a 1902 M.C.C. motion that the bowling crease be increased from seventy-eight inches to eighty inches but refused to give his reason to the Chairman.

D

RICHARD DAFT, Notts., b. 1831, was the last practitioner of the underleg stroke and the art died with him.

MR DARTNELL, *c*. 1867, a Methodist draper of Broad Green, Surrey, took 10 Thornton Heath wkts for 0 runs. And there were no extras.

M.P. DONNELLY, Warwks., 1948, was hit on the foot by a ball from J.C. Young which, bouncing over his wicket, spun back and bowled him from behind.

GEORGE DEARMAN of Sheffield, handsomely defeated in a single wkt game, yet earned a generous encomium from the victor, the Great Mynn, *'for his unflinching bottom'*.

JOHN DERRICK, of Guildford, 1554, by declaring on oath that, at the time of an alleged offence, he was playing cricket, became the first named cricketer.

J.W.H.T. DOUGLAS, Essex and England captain, d. 1930 aged forty-eight while attempting the rescue of his father during shipwreck in the Kattegat. This dour bowler lives on in memory of the seven successive England defeats under his captaincy, the play of words upon his initials and his centre-parted gleaming black hair.

GEORGE DUCKWORTH, Lancs., England, d. 1966, a wicket-keeper, was surpassed in appeals only by Dr Barnardo.

DULEEPSINGHI, Sussex and England, d. 1959, aged fifty-four, a quiet, discerning Indian, who having made fifty centuries in seven and a half seasons, at the age of twenty-seven, was forced by ill-health to play no more. After making 173 on his first appearance against Australia, he was chided for the fatally injudicious stroke by his uncle – *'You make your first* *hundred for your side. And your second hundred for your side. You may then employ the getting of the third hundred as best suits yourself.*

SNOWDEN DUNHILL, Spaldington (East Riding), *c.* 1820, who by the Saving Grace of God and the skills of cricket learned at his dear parents' knees, recovered from a dissipated youth to captain an XI composed of others of his family and in-laws similarly transported to Tasmania. This newborn man's wife set up as a schoolmistress and taught her pupils to bake the cakes sold advantageously between innings.

E

VICTOR EBERLE, d. 1974, was the Clifton schoolboy who dropped Master A.E.J. Collins (*q.v.*) when he had scored only 20.

EDGAR, a racing pigeon employed by Old Ebor of the *Yorkshire Evening Post* to carry his reports, failed in his attempts to become airborne when detailed accounts of Sutcliffe and Leylands' centuries v. Lancashire (1928) were attached to his leg.

EDWARD VII, having been persuaded with immense difficulty to take part in a cricket game, was immediately bowled out by an over-excited East Anglian parson.

TOM EMMETT, Yorks., b. Halifax, 1841, a mournful-looking man, politely asked of an Australian fielder who had crept in close, if he was wed. He explained that, although he had no compunction about killing him, the death of a husband and father would vex his peace of mind. This kindly man bowled fast left-arm 'sostenuters' at the leg-stump and, in his forty-fifth year, bowled 1,339 overs, taking 132 wkts at 12 runs apiece. Later, when Time's fell hand compelled him to coach public-schoolboys, he would urge them to,

'*Smell her, Smell her!*' It was this same Emmett who coined that consoling poetic fancy, '*First a wide. Then a wicket.*'

F

ARTHUR FAGG, Kent, d. 1977, performed the unique feat of making 244 and 202* in the first and second innings against Essex in 1938, at Colchester.

THE REVD. ELISHA FAWCETT, *c.* 1817, a Manchester evangelical who devoted his life to teaching the natives of the Admiralty Islands the Commandments of God and the Laws of Cricket. Too poor to purchase a monument to this good man, his parishioners erected his wooden leg upon his grave. In that fertile clime it miraculously took root and for many years provided a bountiful harvest of bats.

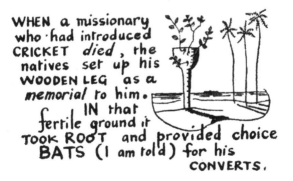

WHEN a missionary who had introduced CRICKET *died*, the natives set up his WOODEN LEG as a *memorial* to him. IN that *fertile* ground it TOOK ROOT and provided choice BATS (I am told) for his CONVERTS.

FELIX, the preferred name of Nicholas Wanostrocht, a Blackheath writing-master, who not only invented tubular gloves and a mechanical bowler, the Catapulta, but wrote the classic tutor, *Felix on the Bat* (which often is to be found in the Natural History Section of public libraries).

NICHOLAS FELIX, Kent, *c.* 1840, kept a note of his score on his starched shirt-front.

THE REVD. WILLIAM FELLOWES, *c.* 1830, an Oxford University chaplain, lately jilted by the Dean of Christ Church's elder daughter, struck a cricket ball 176 measured paces.

P.G.H. FENDER, Surrey, b. 1892, the greatest captain of his time. In 1920, against Northants., he made the fastest century in first-class cricket, in thirty-five minutes.

T.A. FISON, *c.* 1901, Hendon, after reaching 264 v. Highgate School, '*Retired to catch a train to the Continent*'.

F.R. FOSTER, Warwks., b. 1889, a left-arm amateur bowler, who, with the great Barnes, formed the most effective Test-winning bowling partnership.

FREDERICK LOUIS, PRINCE OF WALES, d. 1751, is the only member of the Royal Family known to have died violently after a blow from a cricket ball.

A.P. FREEMAN, Kent, d. 1965; this five-foot-two-inches tall right-arm bowler of leg-breaks, googlies and top-spinners, took 3,776 wkts in his career.

C.B. FRY, Hants., b. 1872, who claimed that he had only one stroke but which he could make go in nine different directions, held the world's long-jump record, played in an F.A. Cup Final, headed the England batting averages in six seasons and was a notable classical scholar. At the Treaty of Versailles it was sensibly proposed that he be crowned King of Albania, a blessing denied that unhappy land which, instead, inherited a family called Zog and, later, went Maoist.

G

HARRY GILL, *c.* 1930, a collier, Captain of Sherburn-in-Elmet C.C. and an admired bass singer of sacred solos, invited this editor, then a schoolboy, to replace a defaulter and play in his first men's game at the last match of the season. He then demonstrated true Gentility and Nobility of Nature by putting *himself* in at No. 11. *Requiescat in pace.*

A.E.R. GILLIGAN, Sussex and England Captain, d. 1976, known also by unlettered northerners as the Revd. A.E.R. Gillingham, made his first first-class century at No. 11. After a blow over the heart, he never again bowled really fast.

THE REVD. CANON F.H. GILLINGHAM, Essex, d. 1953, *See* A.E.R. GILLIGAN.

SIR HORACE GORDON, BART., whose circumstances were such that, gainful employment being needless, devoted himself to increasing the sum of human knowledge by revealing that, between 1881 and 1938, 6,000,508 runs were made in country cricket for the loss of 2,271 wkts, at an average of 23.4 runs per wkt. In less solemn mood, he composed the most beautiful delineation of Cricket's Glorious Edifice –

The spacious foundations are formed by village matches, on them to be raised the charming ground-floor of club cricket. The more austere superstructure of county encounters appears majestic but severe. The cupola consists of Test Matches and is so elevated as to excite ambitious aspiration . . .

and so on.

A.R. Gover, the Surrey Captain, while pulling a sweater over his head, made a catch between his legs, J.C. Laker's first wkt in first-class cricket.

Dr. E.M. Grace, Glos., b. 1841, was so agile in the field that it was said that the only thing he could not do was to keep wicket to his own bowling.

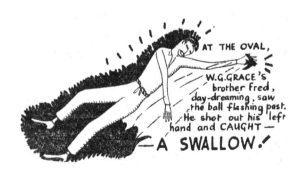

AT THE OVAL, W.G. GRACE'S brother Fred, day-dreaming, saw the ball flashing past. He shot out his left hand and CAUGHT — A SWALLOW!

Mrs Martha Grace, née Pocock, b. 1812, Glos., a handsome, large-featured matriarch who played the harp, is the only woman canonized in *Wisden*. That wayward genius which, in her father, impelled him to invent a kite-drawn, chimney-toppling carriage, manifested itself more fruitfully in her several sons.

Dr William Gilbert Grace, Glos., b. 1848, 'The Champion', 'The Big 'Un', whose portrait in a pre-existence may be seen engraved upon Assyrian tablets in the British Museum. Between 1870 and 1900 this Jove-like folk-hero bestrode the game, the Lillees and Thomsons of his day scarce daring to bowl within his reach. The sole ace to this king was the Australian Spofforth and it is said that, facing the original 'demon bowler', the grinding of Grace's teeth was clearly audible to both umpires. One mere item in this Olympian

W. G. Grace

career – in 1876, during successive innings, he made 344 v. M.C.C., 177 v. Notts, 400 v. a Lincolnshire XXII and 318* v. Yorkshire. He gave the game a new law – 'Braces are not worn.'

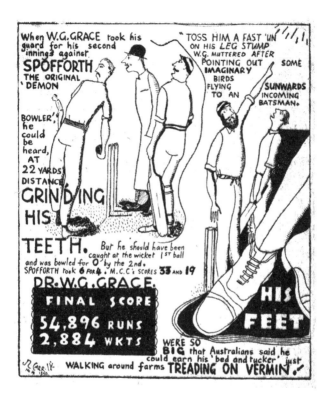

ROBERT GRAVES, poet, during a short interal in the
Battle of Vermelles, 1915, played cricket employing a
rafter as a bat, a rag ball and a wicket simulated by a
birdcage housing the clean corpse of a parrot.

THE HON. ROBT. GRIMSTON, *c.* 1830, a youthful revolutionary who provided himself with two bats, a large one to block Mynn and a smaller one to thrash lesser bowlers, but who, in later life, became a reactionary President of M.C.C., forbidding the introduction of the mowing machine and the expulsion of the Lord's flock of sheep.

MR GRUNDY, *c.* 1910, a Bearsted wheelwright, having been furnished by Edward Thomas, the poet, with a diagram so that he could shape a new wooden leg for the Welsh poet, W.H. Davies, but not having been told what it was, made out the bill 'For a Curiosity Cricket Bat'.

GEORGE GUNN, Notts., b. 1879, a small, slim man, who by taking his stand at varying places, demoralized bowlers. This seemingly immortal player actually did believe that cricket was only a game. On a particularly hot day, observing his wife take her seat in the stands, he immediately got himself out and joined her. In the West Indies he held out a solar topee in his left hand to catch a steepler but, at the last moment, mindful of Rule 41, caught it in his right. He was a fastidious man who, during an innings of 119 at Sydney, claimed that his concentration was disturbed not by the military band but by its solo cornet playing out of tune. His last words were: *'Batsmen take too great a heed of bowlers.'*

H

HARRY HALL, a gingerbread baker of Farnham, takes his place in cricket's Glorious Annals for teaching young Wm. Beldham to keep his left elbow up.

W.R. HAMMOND, Glos., b. 1903 at Dover, a sound yet daringly brilliant bat who made 50,493 runs (av. 56) and 167 centuries. Whilst facing the hitherto devastating Australian fast bowler, Macdonald, he invested his drives with such executionary vigour that the ball frequently bounced from the fence half-way back to the wicket.

SAMUEL HARPER, Thorne Colliery Nightjars, made 100 in fourteen minutes while his partner contributed 2. This feat was vouched for (in writing) by Sir Archibald White.

GEORGE HARPOLE, *c.* 1949, of Tampling, struck a ball upon the bent back of his runner who unwittingly carried it into the hands of a mid-off.

LORD HARRIS, President of the Kent County Cricket Club, b. 1851, was the man who actually saw the Australian, Ernest Jones's ball pass through W.G. Grace's beard.

IN THE EARLY DAYS OF CRICKET, DAVID HARRIS OF HAMBLEDON BOWLED UNDERARM SO FAST THAT A **BYE** KILLED A DOG ON THE BOUNDARY. HIS DELIVERIES WERE SO TERRIFYING THAT THE **LONG-STOP** USED TO WEAR A BAG OF **HAY**. NO WONDER HAMBLEDON BEAT **ENGLAND.**

DAVID HARRIS, b. Elvetham, 1754, a potter, the most feared underarm bowler of his age, it being said that '*his fatal expression before delivery was appalling*'. First raising the ball to his brow he pistoned it from beneath his armpit causing it to leap steeply and bloodily grind fingers into bat handle. This formidable man, brushing aside a gouty old age, supported himself on a crutch and, between overs, rested upon an armchair set up behind the wickets.

LORD HAWKE, Yorks., b. 1860, Captain 1883–1910, President 1898–1938, during whose reign the Championship was won 20 times. Part warlord, part folkhero, he instituted winter pay and

partial investment of benefit money to ensure a decent living for professional players.

TOM HAYWARD, b. Cambridge, 1871. This Surrey batsman was the second player to make 100 centuries.

DR HEATH, D.D., Headmaster of Eton, a perfectionist, flogged the School XI, including (possibly unjustly) the scorer, when they returned from a defeat by Westminster School.

ELIAS HENDREN, Mddx., b. 1889, a stockily built man of mordant wit who scored ducks in his first and last county games but, between, made 57,611 runs and 170 centuries.

GEORGE HERBERT HIRST, Yorks., b. Kirkheaton, 1871. His inswinger was described as a hard and accurate throw from cover-point and his 1906 feat of 208 wkts and 2,385 runs is unsurpassed. He modestly attributed a figment of his fame to the use of neats-foot oil and is the subject of the game's most eloquent poem –

> *When I faced the bowling of Hirst*
> *I called out, 'Do your worst.'*
> *He answered, 'Right you are Sid.'*
> *And he did.*

JOHN BERRY HOBBS, b. Cambridge, 1882, the eldest of a net-bowler's twelve children. This shrewd, lean Surrey player, a man of great natural dignity and forceful elegance of stroke, was the bridge between the Classic and Modern Periods. He made 61,237 runs (av. 50) and his knighthood was joyfully acclaimed by the nation.

PERCY HOLMES, Yorks., d. 1971, an unusually straight-backed opening bat who, in 1925, scored 2,453 runs. As he made his jaunty way from pavilion to wicket, discerning spectators received an impression that he was off for a day at the races, whilst his partner, Herbert Sutcliffe, had been called upon to lay an aldermanic stone. He once described an innings on a broken, dusty pitch as like batting on Blackpool sands.

HORACE, *c.* 1890, a horse of such exquisite sensibility that, when Fred Morley, the invariable Notts. last man, left the Trent Bridge pavilion, it sidled unobtrusively towards the roller.

ALBERT HORNBY, amateur, b. Blackburn, 1847 and Richard Barlow, professional, b. Bolton, 1850, the *'run-stealers'* who *'flickered to and fro'*, linked till eternity in cricket's only Eng. Lit. Div. One's poem.

LORD HOWE, b. 1726, whose father died of drinking coconut milk in Barbados, gave his name to a Pacific island of 150 souls yet fielding two XIs compelled to have fixtures only with one another, and on a ground so contiguous with the ocean that wickets could be pitched only at one end, the batsmen swapping places for the strike.

SIR LEONARD HUTTON, Yorks., b. 1916, an opening bat of high art and gritty resolve, who surged to fame by making 365 against Bradman's 1938 Test side at the Oval. His career was crowned by the very successful appointment as England's first professional captain in modern times.

J

THE HON. F.S. JACKSON, b. 1870, Chairman of the Conservative Party. In the 1905 Tests he won the toss five times, won the series, won the batting (70.2) and bowling averages (15.4). Despairing of ambition's chiefest prize, the Yorkshire captaincy, he took to politics and was consoled with the Governorship of Burma. There he escaped an assassin's sword by *'the quickest duck I ever made'*.

JOHN JACKSON, Notts., a shy man, customarily blew his nose loudly in embarrassment after clean-bowling batsmen. In Derbyshire, he was known unkindly as Foghorn.

D.R. JARDINE, Surrey, d. 1958, sailed for Australia in 1932 to bring back the Ashes. And he did.

GILBERT JESSOP, Glos., b. Cheltenham, 1874, a shortish man, dreaded by the Civil Service Commissioners and Merchant Banks as the most  effective office-emptier in history, his average hourly scoring-rate being 80 runs. He *assaulted* bowling, redirecting balls like stones from a catapult. His 1902 innings of 104 in 77 minutes when England, needing 200, were 48 for 5 can only be compared with Henry V's speech before Harfleur. His cricket career ended in 1916 when he was forgotten in a heat-treatment box.

K

ALBERT KETTLEWELL, at Bramall Lane and suffering the scratchings-around of the public-school-coached scion of an illustrious council-school-playground-reared father, in a godlike excess of rage and mindful of his County's Glorious Past, uprose and roared, *'Fetch thi' Dad!'* This editor, his neighbour, while secretly admitting the justice of his plea, basely shrank from him.

ROY KILNER, Yorks., d. 1928, aged thirty-eight. This all-rounder (1,000 runs, 100 wkts on four occasions), died at Barnsley from enteric fever caught while coaching in India. He made the ultimate pronouncement on the Roses games – *'Let there be no umpires and then Fair Cheating all round.'*

ALBERT KNIGHT, Leics., c. 1903, customarily knelt and prayed at the crease before receiving a first delivery.

CHARLES JESSE KORTRIGHT, Essex, b. 1891, by aficionados said to have been the fastest bowler of them all. Having witnessed W.G. Grace's refusal to go when caught from what he claimed was a bump-ball, he subsequently flattened two stumps, crying ironically, *'Why are you going? There's still one stump standing.'*

L

JAMES LAKER, Surrey, but born Bradford, bowled accurate, high-action, bouncy finger-clicking off-spinners. In the 1950 Test Trial on a sympathetic Yorkshire wicket, he took 8 wkts for 2 runs. (Half of which were made by F.S. Trueman). In the 1956 Old Trafford Test v. Australia, he performed the astonishing feat of taking 19 wkts for 90 runs.

MR LAMBOURN, 'The Littel Farmer', Hambledon, *c.* 1770, invented underarm spin and the off-break and sapped batsmen's morale by crying, *'Ah! That was tedious near you, Sir!'*

HAROLD LARWOOD, Notts., b. 1904, a quiet pitman, the greatest fast bowler of his Age, summoned by Time to eclipse the lustrous Bradman. His onslaught was so

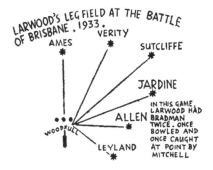

LARWOOD'S LEG FIELD AT THE BATTLE OF BRISBANE, 1933.
AMES
VERITY
SUTCLIFFE
JARDINE
WOODFULL
ALLEN
LEYLAND

IN THIS GAME, LARWOOD HAD BRADMAN TWICE. ONCE BOWLED AND ONCE CAUGHT AT POINT BY MITCHELL

projectile that his knuckles sometimes grazed the pitch. Given this book by Nottingham Rotarians, he murmured, '*He's got this bit about Hammond wrong.*'

GEORGE LEER, Hambledon, *c.* 1770, a brewer, whose long-stopping was said to be safe as a sandbank. While awaiting incoming batsmen he sang glees with his wicket-keeper (a tenor) in a high alto voice.

MR LEESTON-SMITH, Somerset, hit W.G. Grace for four successive sixes at Weston-Super-Mare. The umpire, having said '*I'm afraid it's over, Doctor,*' was told to shut up. And the seventh ball had him stumped.

GEORGE LENNOX, 4th Duke of Richmond, like the immortal Wolfe, ascended the Heights of Abraham but to play cricket. In a duel he shot off a curl from the Prince Regent's proxy, the Duke of York. And it was his beautiful wife who gave the celebrated Eve of Waterloo Ball at Quatre Bras (*see* Eng. Lit.). He died from hydrophobia after a fox-bite.

MAURICE LEYLAND's (Yorks., d. 1967) bat was but a natural extension of his arms and bottle-necked shoulders. This stout-hearted and sturdily built midlist damage-repairer made 1,705 runs against Australia (av. 57) and his emergence from the pavilion at No. 5 acutely depressed their side, because as A.A. Mailey complained, '*It was as if the innings was beginning all over again.*' For a left-hander, he had an unusually frank face. His *obiter dicta* – '*None of us like really fast bowlers. But we don't all let on.*'

WILLIAM LILLYWHITE, b. 1792, West Hampnett, Sussex, 'The Nonpareil', a dapper fiercely small man, first to take 100 wkts in a season. After reflection, he made the Ultimate Pronouncement – '*I suppose if I was to think* every *ball, nobody'd ever get a run.*'

MRS EMMA LOCKSLEY, landlady of the New Lord's Tavern, in a fit of despair, blew up her house, her sister-in-law and herself.

THE WEATHER VANE ON THE PAVILION AT **LORDS** SHOWS FATHER **TIME** DRAWING STUMPS.

Thomas Lord, b. Thirsk, 1755, a Jacobite, bought his first ground in Dorset Square in 1787. He died at West Meon, Hants.

'**Miss Flora Lynn**', *c.* 1890, Captain of the Original Lady Cricketers, dared not reveal her secret addiction during her husband, Mr Westbrook's, lifetime.

The Fourth Lord Lyttelton's eight sons played for Worcestershire, yet, between them, produced only one county player. It was his custom to visit jumble sales to buy back his older garments donated by his wife.

M

Francis MacKinnon, the Thirty-fifth MacKinnon of MacKinnon, b. 1848, played in the first Test in Australia, and made 0 and 0.

A.C. MacLaren, Lancs., d. 1944, was a magnifico who disconcertingly awaited a bowler's worst with a high-uplifted bat. As he hovered beneath an Australian's skier, he was made a most remarkable offer: – *'Miss it, Archie, and you can kiss me big sister.'*

Noah Mann, *c.* 1770, Hambledon, a gypsy inn-keeper, inventor of swerve bowling, entertained early arrivals at games by daring bareback riding feats and died by falling on a fire while not himself.

Mr Marcon, *c.* 1884, an Oxford University bowler, by methods which he was unwilling to divulge, made his deliveries leap so high and unpredictably that two long-stops were needed: one to stun the ball and one to kill it.

J. Martison, *c.* 1921, of Eastrington, nr. Selby, opened the innings against Cliffe Common and carried his bat for 0 when Mr Tune took 10 wkts for 0 runs.

P.B.H. May, Cambridge University and Mddx., b. 1929, a sagacious and determined England Captain, who has been described as an amateur with a professional approach. He was a truly great on-driver and in the 1957 Edgbaston Test v. West Indies, shared a partnership of 411 with C. Cowdrey.

Phillip Mead, Hants., 1887, a left-handed awkward-looking bat who made 153 centuries, inspiring the immortal headline HANTS COLLAPSES, MEAD STILL BATTING. When, in the 1930s his County Committee gave £1 talent money for 50 runs plus, he would accumulate these and remark, drily, *'Well, that's another ton of coal to see us through winter.'* He bore his later blindness with great fortitude.

A.A. Milne, d. 1956, the celebrated author, now and then confounded batsmen by delivering balls from behind and over the heads of umpires.

Miss Mary Mitford, d. 1855, by her literary labours, supported a father who had squandered her mother's fortune: her account in *Our Village* of the preparation for a match between local rivals is delightful. She paid Woman's most felicitous

tribute to cricket: '*Who would think a little bit of leather and two pieces of wood had such delighting and delightful powers?*'

The Rev. Mr Mitford, *c.* 1800, bidding a farewell to the Hambledon XI, idolatrously kissed Wm. Beldham's bat and, thus inspired, misquoted Ecclesiastes, Chap. i, v.2, '*Vanity of vanities, saith the Preacher, vanity of vanities: all is vanity save Cricket.*'

Miss Rose Morphy, *c.* 1882, a beautiful Australian wit, having burned a bail to Ashes, on presenting the urn to the English captain, the Hon. Ivo Bligh, immediately fell in love and married him.

Alfred Mynn, b. Goudhurst, 1807, The Lion of Kent, Alfred the Great, a farmer's boy, later a hop merchant. The majestic round-armers delivered by this noble twenty-stone fellow nipped from leg to off stump, requiring the presence of stumper and long-stops-in-tandem. His spirit was great as his person for, while making 146 v. the North, he was so grievously hammered on his unpadded forward leg that it was

Alfred Mynn

feared that he must lose it, exciting even the pity of Lord Beauclerk. Properly he is the subject of the game's most fulsome verse panegyric and is the only cricketer to have been heard of in France, where he was hailed, '*Voila le Grand Mynn!*'

N

HESKETH K. NAYLER, *c.* 1851, a New York millionaire impotent who derived sexual gratification by maintaining an establishment of ample women to play cricket before him with balloons and without clothes.

SIR HENRY NEWBOLT, Staffs., b. 1862, wrote cricket's best-known literary allusion. Nevertheless, his *'a bumping pitch and a blinding light'*, shamelessly misinterpreted by countless English masters, has caused numerous schoolboys, in hope of having their captain's hand on their shoulder smote, mildly to accept assaults from fast bowlers, rather than assaulting the groundsman.

MR NEWMAN, Hants., having failed in an appeal against bad light, responded, to his partner, Lord Tennyson's *'Can you hear me, Newman?'* with *'Yes, my Lord, but where are you speaking from?'*

MR NIXON, *c.* 1823, a benefactor, rid the world of the painful affliction of stingers by inventing the cane-handled bat.

NORTHAMPTONSHIRE
COUNTY CRICKET LEAGUE

1961

RICHARD NYREN, b. 1734, Jacobite landlord of the Bat
& Ball Inn overlooking Halfpenny Down, cricket's
Olympus. He was a big, independent man, Captain-

General of Hambledon in its Heroic Age and sold ale at 2d a pint which 'flared like turpentine'.

JOHN NYREN, b. 1764, son of Richard, a large bald and bullet-headed man with deeply sunk eyes, cricket's Herodotus: his *Young Cricketer's Tutor* and *Cricketers of My Time* are the Old Testament and Apocrypha of the game. He was a friend of the musician, Novello and the bookwriter Lamb, and was an Admirer of the Noble and Good in Art and Nature.

John Nyren

He composed the glee, 'Come Fill the Goblet' (words by Byron), played the fiddle and was extremely fond of black Kent cherries.

George Osbaldeston, b. 1786, Squire of Hutton Buscell, nr. Scarborough, Master of the Pytchley and Quorn Hunts, batted as well on four legs as most men on two.

A.N. Other, a willing, but unskilled player, when not employed making up village and country-house sides, frequently undertakes off-stage roles in romantic theatrical performances where heroines crush hope in swelling hearts by crying out that they love A.N. Other.

P

GEORGE PARR, b. Radcliffe-on-Trent, 1884, whose towering pulls having so often battered a tree on the Trent Bridge leg-boundary, felicitously a bough from this same tree was borne upon his bier.

EDDIE PAYNTER, Lancs., a cheerfully dauntless left-hander who, in a single 1937 day, made 322 v. Sussex.

ROBERT PEEL, Yorks, when not himself, was sacked by Lord Hawke for mistaking the pavilion for a batsman and bowling at it.

RICHARD PERCEVAL, Durham, *c.* 1884, threw a ball 140 yards, two feet.

FULLER PILCH, b. Horningtoft, Norfolk, 1803 but a Kent player, is said to have had so fantastically long a reach that he cast a despairing blight on opposing sides. In retirement he kept the Saracen's Head, Canterbury, refusing all appeals for credit as, umpiring, he did for lbw (scornfully crying, *'Bowl 'em out!'*).

In 1875 Mr Brown of Bishop Aukland bet £20 to £10 that a Mr Piers could not bowl him out in **12 HOURS.** He used a bat **10 inches** wide. Piers found a pot ball weighing **27** ounces. The bat soon splintered and Brown lost his nerve and drew away. All **3** wickets were shattered in **9½ MINUTES !**

MR PIERS, *c.* 1875, Bishop Auckland, had a pot ball of twenty-seven ounces baked when challenged by a Mr Brown to bowl him out within six hours (he having manufactured a bat so wide that he was able to stand behind it). The contest ended when, after nine and a half minutes, Brown's nerve and bat were shattered.

PONTO, *c.* 1850, the bravest of the Grace Family's dogs who, fielding close-in, fearlessly presented his breast to drives and, in the out-orchard, sagaciously plotted the path of approaching balls from crashing branches.

THE REVD. CHARLES POWLETT, *c.* 1760, Vicar of Itchen Abbass, son of the Duke of Bolton and Lavinia Fenton (the original Polly Peachum) founded the Hambledon Club.

Q

W.G. QUAIFE, Warwks., b. 1872, was the archetypal text-book bat.

JL CARR. No.12.

R

RANJITSINHJI, Maharajah Jam Sahib of Nawanagar, Sussex, b. 1872, whose elegant yet aggressive cutting, leg glides, race and title, captured the nation's imagination. Why, even my father had heard of him.

MASTER REDFERN, *c.* 1899, a Clifton schoolboy who, going in last, shared a partnership of 187 to which he contributed 13. (*See* MASTER COLLINS.)

WILFRED RHODES, Yorks., b. 1877, took 4,187 wkts and made 39,802 runs. He first played for England before seven players in the 1926 Test, his last, were born, yet his bowling retained its subtle flight and impeccable length. For the last twenty years of his life this great man was blind. One can only marvel at a recently notorious list of peerages knowing that he never received one.

TOM RICHARDSON, Surrey, b. 1870, declared by many to have been the greatest fast bowler. Using a vicious breakback, in four seasons he took 1,005 wkts at 14 runs apiece. This great-hearted man petitioned Authority to introduce ten-ball overs.

R.C. Robertson-Glasgow, Oxford University & Somerset, d. 1965, known also as Crusoe, an *Observer* miniaturist, had so loud a voice that when in the district, he was recruited by the Bishop's Lydeard choirmaster to put down a dissident bass butcher, who, from a front pew, perversely drowned the official choir.

Valentine Russell, Wimbledon, *c.* 1903, was the handsomest man the cricket field has ever known and it was not uncommon for ladies to pay for entrance purely (one supposes) to gaze at him. Consequently, he was much sought after for charity matches and customarily was sent to field on the boundary's edge at both ends.

REMODELLING WELLINGBOROUGH GROUND

S

Hugh de Selincourt, b. 1878, Captain of Storrington village, in 1924 published *The Cricket Match*, his masterpiece, a charming melodrama enclosed in a single hot August day.

E.H.D. Sewell is the only man to have been no-balled for a delivery whilst performing levitation.

SCORE BOOKS WERE **CHEAP** IN EARLIER DAYS. THE SCORERS CUT A **NOTCH** IN THE GREEN BARK OF ASH BOUGHS AND MARKED EACH **10TH RUN** BY A DEEPER CUT. IN YORKSHIRE A BATSMAN IS STILL ASKED HOW MANY HE **NOTCHED**.

MR SEXTON, an Essex farmer, owned a magnificent *salix alba* from which 1,179 bats were manufactured.

WILLIAM SHAKESPEARE, Warwks., d. 1616, when penning the lines, '*Some men are born great, some achieve greatness and some have greatness thrust upon them*', may not have had M.A. Nash, Glamorgan, particularly in mind. Nevertheless, he is the third classification made flesh, for it was from one of his overs at Swansea in 1968 that G.S. Sobers, the West Indian, hit six sixes.

ALFRED SHAW, Notts. & Sussex, the most accurate length-bowler in history, ascribed his feat of 17,000 maidens out of 25,000 overs to beginning working life as a bird-scarer.

GEORGE BERNARD SHAW, an author, on being told England had been successful in the Australian Tests enquired what they had been testing.

J.C. SHAW, Notts., b. 1837, height five feet nine inches, weight twelve stones nine pounds, a left-armed, high-action, fast bowler, during the season of 1867, delivered 9,876 balls to garner 450 wkts. On dismissing a batsman it was his practice to plunge both hands deep into his trouser pockets and to assume an unusually vacant facial expression. He was so awful a bat that he holds the first-class cricket record for going in last man.

THE RIGHT REVD. D.H. SHEPPARD, Lord Bishop of Liverpool, d. 2005, while yet at the University of Cambridge, topped the first-class batting averages with 64.67 runs per innings.

ARTHUR SHREWSBURY, Notts., b. New Lenton, 1856, a batsman of determination and artistry, in his day second only in reputation to W.G. Grace. No one ever saw the top of his head, which on the field he concealed by a cap; off it, by a bowler, and in his bed, with a night-cap. Believing himself afflicted by an incurable disease, he shot himself and lies twenty-two yards from that great bowler, J.C. Shaw.

G.H.J. SIMPSON-HAYWARD was the last lob-bowler to play regularly for his county. At Worcester in 1909, employing underarms, he took 6 Australian wkts for 142.

ALEC SKELDING, an umpire, who in 1932 at Sheffield with Horace Fisher, bowling left-arm slows, adjudicated in favour of two successive appeals for lbw. When the third ball struck the legs of one, W.T. Luckes, Somerset, he again raised his forefinger, pronouncing solemnly, '*As God is my witness, that is Out also.*'

A. Skelding, Leics., (*c.* 1920), a bowler, wore spectacles which invariably misted up so densely that he was able only to see both batsman and wickets as through a glass darkly. He thus was compelled to appeal twice an over just in case.

John Small, Hambledon, b. Petersfield, 1737, a cobbler and choirman. During his innings of two and three-quarter hours on 22 May 1775, while making the 14 runs to defeat England, it was observed that three balls passed between his two stumps, making necessary the fatal institution of the middle wicket. His epitaph begins thus –

> *Here bowled by Death's unerring ball*
> *A cricketer renowned by name John Small.*

THE REVD. ELISHA SMITH, Towcester, *c.* 1773, at the age of nineteen renounced loose living, dancing and cricket, '*the last of which he was particularly fond*'.

SIR AUBREY SMITH, Oxford University and Hollywood, Ca., known also as 'Round-the-Corner Smith', in 1883, bowling high-arm cutters evolved from logarithmically based curves, took 6 Cambridge wkts for 78 runs. Progressing triumphantly from one Theatre of Fame to another, his cinematographic performances in *The Prisoner of Zenda* and *The Garden of Allah*, were surpassed only by an earlier illusion that the wind always blew from whichever end he happened to be bowling.

MESSRS SPIERS & POND, Caterers, forced to cancel the 1861 Australian literary lecture tour by the popular novelist Charles Dickens, substituted the first England cricket tour to the Antipodes and made a profit of £12,000.

SIR JOHN SQUIRE, d. 1958, editor of the *London Mercury* and a poetry anthologist, ran a touring side named the Invalids and customarily bowled (unchanged) slow left-handers '*to keep the batsman happy*'.

A.E. STODDART, Mddx., b. 1863, captained England at cricket and rugby. He was an athlete nonpareil, who, after making 485 in an afternoon match for Hampstead v. the Stoics, played some sets of tennis before joining a junior party which continued to the theatre. His 173 at Melbourne (1894), was the highest score by an English skipper for eighty years and an Australian journal imagined Queen Victoria murmuring, '*I must do something for my dear victorious Stod.*' He made 221 v. Somerset in his last first-class game and, in 1915, shot himself.

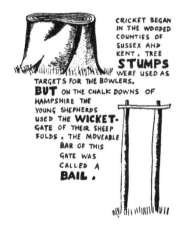

CRICKET BEGAN IN THE WOODED COUNTIES OF SUSSEX AND KENT . TREE **STUMPS** WERE USED AS TARGETS FOR THE BOWLERS. **BUT** ON THE CHALK DOWNS OF HAMPSHIRE THE YOUNG SHEPHERDS USED THE **WICKET-**GATE OF THEIR SHEEP FOLDS . THE MOVEABLE BAR OF THIS GATE WAS CALLED A **BAIL** .

THE REVD. THOS. STURGESS-JONES, Rector of Garboldisham, *c.* 1922, an advanced thinker, fearlessly published the village side's averages in his parish magazines.

MR SUGNETT, a Croydon headmaster, *c.* 1893, described as '*a destructive-looking man*', customarily improved his fast underarm grubs by following them down the pitch yelling fiercely, '*That's gotyer!*'

HERBERT SUTCLIFFE, Yorks., d. 1978, an elegant resourceful partner in the best opening pair England ever had. In the 1924 Australian Tests, his average score was 81.5.

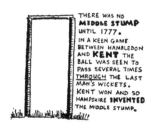

THERE WAS NO **MIDDLE STUMP** UNTIL 1777. IN A KEEN GAME BETWEEN HAMBLEDON AND **KENT** THE BALL WAS SEEN TO PASS SEVERAL TIMES <u>THROUGH</u> THE LAST MAN'S WICKETS. KENT WON AND SO HAMPSHIRE **INVENTED** THE MIDDLE STUMP.

T

FRED TATE, Sussex, playing in his only Test (1902), dropped an easy catch from Darling (Australia's top scorer), and going in last when England needed but a handful to win, swung and missed. Found weeping in the pavilion, he was not comforted by the ancient lie, '*It's only a game, Fred.*'

MAURICE TATE, b. 1895, took 2,783 wkts (av. 18) and was the greatest medium-fast bowler of his era. He never bowled a no-ball, and his single wide was a floater carried off by the wind. Arms semaphoring, his final footfall struck the turf so hard that cover-points reported slight earth-shocks. His best ball was an outswinger which moved in line of middle and off but, at the last instant, swerved outwards. His *unplayable* ball was this ball bowled in a Brighton sea-fret.

WM. TEMPLE (Headmaster of Repton School). His definition of cricket as organized loafing was not considered sufficient reason to prevent his preferment as Archbishop of Canterbury.

IN THE 3ᴿᴰ TEST, 1921 v. AUSTRALIA THE ENGLAND CAPTAIN, **LORD TENNYSON** WAS BADLY INJURED WHILST FIELDING. **BUT** HOLDING THE BAT WITH **ONE HAND** HE SCORED **63** AGAINST THE FAST BOWLING OF **GREGORY & MACDONALD.**

LIONEL, LORD TENNYSON, Hants., b. 1889, leading England into the jaws of Warwick Armstrong at Leeds, 1921, bravely advanced with one arm in a sling and, wielding his bat like a tennis racquet, volleyed 63 thunderous runs, a glorious feat of arm (all the world wondered). His sole literary work is entitled *From Verse to Worse* and his favourite reading was 'Hiawatha', which he insisted had been written by his grandfather.

GEORGE THWAITES, *c.* 1923, playing in a Monk Fryston meadow, hit a ball into a thick clump of nettles, locally notorious for their fierce sting and subsequently bitter and long-lasting rash. Although lost ball was called, the batsman deviated from his course between the pitched stumps to point out first the ball and then the Unalterable Law that thus it could not be a lost ball. He then returned to complete 189 self-counted runs before a fielder's father fetched his scythe.

MR EDWIN TITCHMARSH, Herts., was so desirous that his infant son should become a first-class county umpire, that he was christened Valentine Adolphus. And he became one.

IN THE EARLY DAYS OF CRICKET THE SIDE WHICH WON THE TOSS CHOSE THE WICKET.

THIS CAUSED FIERCE QUARRELS

BETWEEN *BATSMEN* AND *BOWLERS* OF THE *SAME* SIDE !

UEL TITLEY, a cricket correspondent, d. 1973, was given his unique name by his father, Samuel Titley, who declared, *'Everybody calls me "Sam". The lad can have the other half'*.

A.A. THOMPSON, b. 1894, a Harrogate bookwriter, and sought-after after-dinner speaker, entitled his autobiography *Pavilioned in Splendour* ('and girded with praise', *The Methodist Hymnal*, No. 8).

GEORGE MACAULEY TREVELYAN, O.M., d. 1962, historian, declared, *'If the French noblesse had been capable of playing cricket with their peasants their chateaux would never have been burnt.'*

MR TREVOR and **MR VERNON**, playing for Orleans versus Rickling (Essex) in an afternoon game, made scores of 338 and 250 out of a team total of 920 thrashed from 293 four-ball overs. Rickling did not bat.

A.E. TROTT, 'Albatrott', an Australian who developed a prodigious break by incessantly spinning balls past a packing-case labelled G. Giffen. He joined Middlesex and, in 1907, v. Somerset, took 4 wkts in four balls and, later, performed a hat-trick. His was the only blow which propelled a ball over the present Lord's Pavilion. In 1914, after making a will on a laundry-list, and leaving his entire estate, a wardrobe and £4 to his

landlady, he shot himself. He lies in Plot 613, an unmarked grave in the Willesden Cemetery.

FREDERICK SEWARD TRUEMAN, Yorks., known also as Fiery Fred, bowled, blasted and terrified out 2,304 batsmen during his first-class cricket career. In a 1952 Test v. India, employing this comprehensive battery, he took the first four wickets without a run being scored. It is said that, if invited, he can recite his 307 Test victims in decent chronological order.

JOHN TUNNICLIFFE, Yorks., known also as Long John, shared an opening partnership of 554 with J.T. Brown at Chesterfield in 1898. This Methodist preacher was greatly favoured by my grandfather (who scarcely knew one end of a bat from the other), because of his eloquent denunciation of strong drink.

U

GEORGE ULYETT, Yorks., b. 1851, known also as Happy
Jack, was greatly valued on M.C.C. tours for his feel-
ing whistling solos. Challenged in his opinion that
baseball was a mere children's sport, he knocked 162*
off the United States' foremost pitcher.

HEDLEY VERITY, Yorks., b. Leeds 1905, Rhodes's spiritual heir, in 1932 took 10 Notts. wkts for 10 runs after this editor, then a schoolboy, had left the Headingley ground fearing rain and thus condemning him to a lifetime of bitter remorse. This splendid man, a lieutenant of the Green Howards, terribly wounded, dying and supported by a Bridlington man, was last seen amid blazing Sicilian corn.

THE VICAR OF EASTWOOD, Warwks., *c.* 1870, having married, was told that he no longer could use the vicarage as the cricket club-house.

JASPER VINALL, *c.* 1624, Horstead Keynes, Sussex, was killed while properly preventing an opponent from having two hits at the same ball.

CAPTAIN VINEGAR, b. Millwall, *c.* 1744, owner of a bruisers' agency much employed by cricket game promoters to put down hooligans.

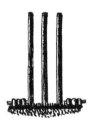

W

TED WAINWRIGHT, Yorks., 1865, customarily slept with his bat.

Tom Walker, Hambledon, *c.* 1770, 'Old Everlasting', once faced the dreaded Harris for 170 balls while making one run. It is said that his skin was like the rind of an ancient oak and, though frequently split, never let blood. Nevertheless, his grunts, like a broken-winded horse, caused great distress among spectators.

Old Wat, a Swaledale sheepdog who, with Mr Trumper of Harefield, defeated Two Gentlemen of Middlesex in 1827. Scores – Two Gents: 1st inns, 3 (both run out), 2nd inns, 3 (both run out). Mr Trumper: 3 (and 2 for his dog), 2nd inns: 2*.

Norman Waterworth, *c.* 1939, Captain/Secretary of Gisburn C.C. was the most committed village player of all time. Having but one leg, he yet took more than 1,000 wkts and made 3,600 runs in twenty-two seasons.

Mr P. Welbourn, Hon. Sec. of the East Molesley Club, politely yet firmly demanded of the opposing captain that he take off Mr Heniker-Gottley because he was being hit so frequently into the River Thames that the club's water-spaniel had refused to recover further balls.

G. WELLS, Sussex, *c.* 1869, was so alarmed at the preparations made by a fast bowler that he knocked down his wicket before the ball was delivered and was given out.

H.G. WELLS, a prolific author of science-fiction and other works, was son of a Hove part-time china dealer who was the first player in Modern Times (1862), to take 4 for 4 in first-class cricket.

John Welles of SUTTON VALENCE invented round-arm bowling & was no balled to an early martyr's crown.

J.C. WHITE, sometimes known as Farmer White, b. 1891 at Stogumber. This slow left-arm bowler took wickets by guile and persistence and so tranquil was his nature that, when a fielder missed a catch, he only went a little redder.

THOMAS 'SHOCK' WHITE, Reigate, *c.* 1770, was held down by Hambledon players while his immense bat was planed down to an acceptable width. Afterwards all incoming batsmen had to pass their bats through a cast-iron frame.

CHRISTINA WILLES, *c.* 1822, who was prevented by a voluminous skirt from bowling underarms, invented round-arm bowling in a Canterbury barn.

JOHN WILLES, Sutton Valence, employing his sister's innovation at Lord's and being continuously no-balled, was so enraged that he rode off never to play again.

A.C. WILLIAMS, briefly for Yorks., 1919, a twelfth man, substituted for Leicestershire and caught four of his own side.

THE EARL OF WINCHILSEA, a man of enviable moral courage, withdrew from the 1789 England side because of cold weather.

MR E. WINTER, *c.* 1832, mis-cutting a ball, drove the bails deep into flattened cleft stumps and, after some deliberation, was judged to be Not Out.

LORD WINTERTON, *c.* 1846, captained an XI which defeated a Sussex Labourers LVII.

JOHN WISDEN, Kent, b. Brighton, 1826, whose feat of 6 wkts in 6 balls v. The South, 1852, has been equalled only by a Mr Brown of Godmanchester, and Mr Kirkland of Bloxwich. Later, he set up a cigar and cricket ball factory and, in 1864, brought out his *Almanack*, which has furnished intellectual and spiritual sustenance to many generations of right-thinking Englishmen.

ARTHUR WOOD, Yorks., b. 1898, was wicket-keeper in the epic 1938 Oval Test and, going in at 770 for 6, made 53 further additions before giving way to another fellow toiler.

FRANK WOOLLEY, Kent, b. Tonbridge, 1887, was a left-handed bat of harmonious sublimity. He made 58,969 runs, took 2,068 wkts and accommodated 1,011 catches in the most prehensile hands in cricket history. Cricket's noblest testimonial was accorded him: '*Woolley will bat for us in Heaven, and Mozart make music.*'

WILLIAM YARDLEY, a Rugby schoolboy, threw 101
yards with his right and seventy-eight with his left
arm.

MR R.A. YOUNG, b. 1885, a mathematics master at Eton
College who played for England in 1907, published a
learned dissertation arguing that fielding captains
should be given an option of pouring up to 100 gallons
of water upon any part of the pitch.

Z

I. **Zingari**, 1899, a daring boatman who promoted cricket matches on the Goodwin Sands at low tide. He has no known connection with a club of that name, founded 1846, which requires candidates for membership to take their stand in the nets without bat and pads and there to be bowled at by vice-presidents.

" This morning we started a single-wicket match."

J.L. Carr's favourite cricket picture.